Australian Biographical Monographs

12

Australian Biographical Monographs
Series Editor: Scott Prasser

Previous Volumes

1	*Joseph Lyons* *and the Management of Adversity*	Kevin Andrews
2	*Harold Holt* *and the Liberal Imagination*	Tom Frame
3	*Johannes Bjelke-Petersen*	Bruce Kingston
4	*Lindsay Thompson* *Character, Competence and Conviction*	William Westerman
5	*Neville Wran*	David Clune
6	*Robert Menzies* *Man or Myth*	Scott Prasser
7	*Stanley Melbourne Bruce* *Institution Builder*	David Lee
8	*John Grey Gorton* *Australian to the Bootheels:* *The paradoxical life of Gorton*	Paul Williams
9	*Sir Robert Askin*	Paul Loughnan
10	*George Reid*	Luke Walker
11	*Neville Bonner*	Sean Jacobs

Australian Biographical Monographs

12

Sir William McKell

David Clune

Connor Court Publishing

Connor Court Publishing Pty Ltd
PO Box 7257
Redland Bay QLD 4165
sales@connorcourt.com
www.connorcourt.com
Phone 0497-900-685

Printed in Australia

ISBN 9781922449726

Front cover design: Maria Giordano

Front cover picture: Wikipedia Commons.

"Australia will probably never again see the emergence of a public figure of [Sir Willam's] type, and for this, the nation will be very much the poorer."

Nick Greiner, New South Wales Hansard,

15 February 1985

Series overview

The Connor Court *Australian Biographical Series* focusses on important Australian political leaders and other major figures. It seeks to provide an overview for those who are unfamiliar with the subject, and to highlight the person's particular importance, controversies around them and their contribution to Australia's progress.

The monographs are scholarly rather than academic in focus, placing emphasis on a clear narrative, but with careful attention to sources to ensure views expressed are appropriately supported.

The Series was initiated because of the decline in the study of Australian history at our schools and universities and the consequential lack of knowledge or, even worse, distorting of views, of some of Australia's leading historical figures who deserve to be remembered, understood for their achievements, and, as each volume also highlights, their flaws.

It has been some time since there has been a biography of Bill McKell, Labor Premier of New South Wales from 1941-47 and then Governor-General from 1947-1953. The memory has long faded, but his worthwhile achievements, not just for the Labor Party, but for the people of New South Wales deserve our attention. Also deserving of attention is his consensus style of leadership, his respect for the processes of parliament, and his ability to stand up to authoritarians like Jack Lang - another Labor premier of New South Wales who will be covered in this series. Today, Lang is perhaps better remembered, but for his notoriety rather than his achievements. It was McKell who rebuilt the Labor Party after its electoral defeats and fragmentation during the 1930s, brought the party back to its true mission of helping those in need rather than self-serving political crusades, and made Labor worth voting for in 1941 when it returned to office and after.

This new monograph by Dr David Clune OAM is an overdue reminder of the contribution of this great Labor leader. Dr Clune, long-time Manager of the New South Wales Parliament's Research Service and the Parliament's Historian, is able to bring fresh insights and a new appreciation of Bill McKell as both a Labor leader, Premier and a decent man who deserves our respect. It supplements David's other monographs in this series on New South Wales premiers Neville Wran and Jack Lang.

- Scott Prasser

Preface

Sir William McKell first came to my notice through my supervisor at Sydney University, Ken Turner. When I was talking to him as a post-graduate student in the 1970s, Ken said that McKell was the greatest twentieth century New South Wales premier. My interest was piqued: Bill who? I had only heard of Jack Lang. I subsequently realised that the man himself used to come regularly into Parliament House in Macquarie Street where I worked. I approached Sir William, with some trepidation, and found him a welcoming, down-to-earth person. It was the beginning of a valued personal relationship. He sometimes invited me to afternoon tea at his apartment in Sydney's Double Bay and sent the Commonwealth car he was entitled to as an ex-Governor-General to collect me and drop me home. The neighbours were mightily impressed!

My MA thesis was about McKell's country strategy in the 1941 election. I followed up with a PhD on Labor's subsequent 24 years in office, set up by McKell. I have published a number of articles and book chapters about him (see the Select Bibliography). I interviewed McKell with Ken Turner and had many informal conversations with him. I have drawn on all this for the current monograph.

Carl Green and Walter Hamilton read the draft and

provided detailed comments and suggestions for which I am most grateful. At Connor Court, I would once again like to thank Scott Prasser and Anthony Cappello for their support.

My greatest debt is to the late Ken Turner. He patiently mentored me, gave unstintingly of his time and ideas, and became a friend and collaborator.

David Clune

June 2021

In the ranks of twentieth century New South Wales premiers, William John McKell and Neville Wran stand out. Both overcame early lack of opportunity, were outstanding politicians, and left behind an impressive, wide-ranging legacy of reform. Unlike Wran, McKell inherited a party in total disarray which he had to restore. Also unlike Wran, who was more an *ad hoc* reformer, McKell had a program that he was determined to implement. Wran governed in peaceful, prosperous times; McKell was premier during a major war and its aftermath. Personally, Wran was tougher and more aggressive.

McKell's influence on the New South Wales Labor Party was crucial. He transformed it from a party that habitually destroyed itself in office into a party with an ethos of stability, moderate politics, achievement and competent administration. A key part of McKell's legacy was an enduring consciousness in the New South Wales Labor Party's parliamentary and extra-parliamentary wings of the importance of compromise, negotiation and co-operation in the interests of electoral success. Labor was increasingly seen as the natural party of government in New South Wales. Between 1901 and 1941, Labor governed for 12 years; for the rest of the twentieth century it was in office for 42.

McKell was a pragmatist with a purpose. He believed that the implementation of Labor policy and the winning of electoral support could be complementary rather than conflicting goals. In reconciling these two aims he was largely successful – a lesson that was certainly not lost on his successors. Both Neville Wran and Bob Carr invoked the McKell legacy.

Early years[1]

Bill McKell was born at Pambula on the New South Wales south coast on 26 September 1891, the first of the four children of Robert and Martha. The young family soon settled in nearby Candelo where Robert was a successful butcher. Bill had a happy rural childhood, retaining a great affection for the bush for the rest of his life. In 1899, Robert relocated his family to Sydney in the hope of improved work prospects. Once again, he worked as a butcher and the McKells lived in inner Sydney.

In 1901, Robert deserted the family, heading for the West Australian gold fields with another woman. He never saw his first family again. The effect on Bill can be gauged by the fact that for the rest of his life he concealed his father's desertion, claiming that he died young. Bill was forced to become a surrogate father:

> Although he was generally a good-natured man, a bitterness remained throughout his life about the abandonment of his boyhood. He determined to be a more than usually responsible son,

husband and father. His caution, frugality, independence and social conscience stemmed partly from his father's betrayal and from the hardship that resulted.[2]

The McKells moved to Redfern, an impoverished, working-class area. Life became a struggle for existence, with Martha working at various menial tasks such as sewing and taking in laundry. Bill supplemented the meagre family income by working part-time. He attended the local Bourke Street School but left at age 13 because of financial pressure.

Bill's main recreation was sport - he was a talented footballer, cricketer and sprinter. He worked part-time as a bookmaker's clerk, and racing and trotting became lifelong passions. Bill's uncle Herb was a well-known boxer and he followed in the family tradition as a pugilist. On 29 July 1926, while Minister of Justice, McKell fought an exhibition match at a boxing charity night at Sydney Stadium: "Glistening in magenta trunks, he boxed four rounds with Harry Collins, welter and middle-weight champion of Australia. [McKell] stood up well to the deft lead and parry ... He recollected that at the finish he had not in all his life felt sounder in wind and limb".[3]

In 1906, McKell became an apprentice boilermaker at Mort's Dock in Balmain. It was a tough and hazardous trade which meant that he had relatively little trouble obtaining a position. Completing his apprenticeship in 1912, McKell had a number of jobs, including at the New South Wales Government Railway's Eveleigh workshops in Redfern, a short walk from home.

The experience of poverty, uncertainty and harsh social and industrial conditions instilled in McKell a drive for self-improvement and a zeal to ameliorate the abuses he had seen, but also a sense of restraint, a carefulness, and a dislike of instability.

McKell soon became active in the labour movement, where his youthful earnestness and fervour made him a militant. As an apprentice, he organised a rebellion against conditions in a new award which he considered unfair. McKell's intelligence, application and ability ensured he rose rapidly through the ranks of the Boilermakers' Society, becoming Assistant Secretary in 1914. He was a member of the Redfern branch of the Labor Party.

Labor had taken office in New South Wales for the first time in 1910 under James McGowen. Young activists like McKell became impatient with the slow process of give and take that achieving reform in government inevitably involved. He became a member of the radical Industrial Section which took control of the Labor Party at the 1916 Annual Conference. McKell was elected to the State Executive.

The Federal and New South Wales Labor governments supported conscription for overseas service in the First World War, resulting in a split in the Party in 1917. McGowen's successor, William Arthur Holman, and most of the parliamentarians left Labor. Conscriptionist Labor MLAs merged with their former conservative opponents as the Nationalist Party, which formed a government under Holman.[4]

Active in the struggle against conscription, McKell gained valuable experience in public speaking and campaigning. He developed into a competent speaker, if not an inspirational one. McGowen, who was MLA for Redfern, had been expelled from the Labor Party as a conscriptionist. Although McGowen was a fellow boilermaker who had been a mentor, McKell successfully sought Labor preselection and was easily elected on 24 March 1917, polling 66 2 per cent of the primary vote to McGowen's 33.2 per cent. McKell represented Redfern for the rest of his career (in the proportional representation period of 1920-25 as part of the multi-member electorate of Botany).

In 1919, McKell bought a house at 80 Dowling Street, Redfern, that was to be his home for almost three decades. The following year he married Mary "Minnie" Pye. The McKell residence was described in a 1944 newspaper profile as:

> ... a solid, old-fashioned, two-storey brick house,

> built in the Victorian days, when Dowling Street, named after Sir James Dowling, second Chief Justice of New South Wales, was a rather fashionable residential area. Mrs McKell does her own housework and fills in her spare time with war work. She says that the old house is comfortable. And then: 'It is handy to everything. The Cricket Ground is just across the way. So is the racecourse. And we can be in the city in a few minutes'.[5]

The McKells had three children, Betty, Patricia and Bill. In 1933, McKell bought a property near Goulburn, "Kulathirrie", which provided a rural retreat and some security against the vagaries of politics. He purchased a nearby property of 1,400 acres, "Newacres", in 1946, which young Bill eventually took over. McKell was a practical farmer. An article in the *Sydney Morning Herald* in April 1941 praised his pioneering erosion control and reclamation measures on "Kulathirrie".[6]

Member of State Parliament

The 25-year-old McKell had a natural affinity for parliamentary life. He developed formidable debating skills, respected the institution and revelled in the hard work involved in mastery of legislation and procedure. McKell had an incisive, analytical mind and powers of concentration that enabled him to grasp the details of complex legal and financial matters. His speeches consisted of a steady, methodical exposition of the facts rather than Holman-like flights of oratory.

When the Legislative Assembly was sitting at night, rather than ensconcing himself in the bar like many of his colleagues, he spent long and productive hours reading and researching in the Parliamentary Library. This work ethic did not prevent the gregarious and genial McKell from being popular with his colleagues.

McKell's ability soon brought him to the attention of Labor's Leader John Storey, another boilermaker turned politician. Storey encouraged him to study law as labour lawyers were in short supply. To begin his studies, McKell had first to pass a preliminary examination, no small challenge for someone with his truncated education. Through HV Evatt, McKell had met Vere Gordon Childe, a brilliant scholar, political radical and later famous archaeologist. They developed a long-term friendship. Childe coached McKell in logic, psychology, and Latin, enabling him to pass and commence his law studies through the Barristers' Admission Board.[7] On 20 December 1925, McKell was admitted to the Sydney Bar and subsequently built up a successful practice. It brought him useful experience, contacts and a good income. In 1946, he was appointed King's Counsel.

With Storey's support, McKell became Minister

of Justice after Labor won the 1920 election. As in subsequent portfolios, McKell proved to be an exemplary minister. He read his files, signed his papers, was thoroughly conversant with departmental business and was on good terms with his officials without being dominated by them. In Cabinet, McKell was always across his brief. He left a legacy of worthwhile reforms behind him in each position he occupied.[8]

For McKell, politics was a means of achieving positive, constructive outcomes. It was not about ego, power or the destruction of enemies. He was a vigorous but not vindictive opponent who had friends on both sides of the chamber. McKell's distaste for divisiveness made him an opponent of the sectarianism that poisoned New South Wales politics in the early decades of the twentieth century. An Anglican, his family included both Catholics and Protestants.

McKell's natural caution and experience of Labor's internal struggles made him reluctant to become involved in faction-fighting. All too often, he had seen the victors in one conflict become the victims in the next. Although ambitious, McKell preferred to succeed through hard work and ability rather than intrigue or manipulation. Maturity and exposure to the realities of achievement through parliamentary politics mellowed the youthful militant. McKell retained a burning sense of injustice about social problems and working-class deprivation. However, he was now committed to the moderate parliamentary road to remedy them.

Surviving Lang

McKell's rise continued – although more uncertainly — under Jack Lang's leadership. An ally but not an intimate of Lang, McKell returned to the Justice portfolio when Labor took office in 1925. He also became Lang's Assistant Minister at Treasury which gave him a valuable insight into public finance. The Premier was wary of the younger man but could see the advantage in using his abilities. McKell, in turn, knew that his career would go nowhere without Lang's support.

Lang's devious, domineering style, his vengefulness towards those who crossed him, and his propensity to claim credit for all the Government's achievements quickly lost him the support of most of his colleagues. In May 1927, he reconstructed his Cabinet with hand-picked loyalists. McKell at first retained his post but was dropped on 8 June for his lack of public enthusiasm for the "Big Fella". Lang used his enormous influence with Labor's rank and file to deprive many of his opponents of their pre-selections. He gave McKell the benefit of the doubt and, assisted by substantial personal support in his branches, McKell kept his endorsement and was re-elected when Labor lost office in October 1927.

When Lang won the October 1930 election, McKell became a minister but was relegated to the minor portfolio of Local Government. Characteristically, he turned the situation to his advantage by proposing a plan for a Greater Sydney Council. Although it never came to fruition, the scheme attracted such favourable publicity that Lang claimed the credit for originating it.

In June 1931, Justice Minister Joe Lamaro became New South Wales Agent-General in London. McKell returned to his former portfolio, where he remained until Lang's dismissal by Governor Game in May 1932. He was one of the few Labor MLAs to retain his seat in the ensuing landslide defeat. Surviving Lang had been a bruising time for the young McKell. However, it left him battle-hardened in the byzantine and devious ways of politics.

Opposition Leader

Growing resentment at Lang's lack of electoral success — the Labor Party had made virtually no headway at the 1935 and 1938 elections — and at his autocratic control, led to open revolt in the labour movement. There were two main forces in the opposition to Lang:

covert Communists who sought to increase their power in the Labor Party, and a group of anti-Lang and anti-Communist union officials whose objective was to restore Labor as a viable electoral force. The latter group supported McKell as the best hope of achieving their aim.

A breakaway Industrial Labor Party was formed in February 1938, led by MLA for Botany Bob Heffron, with the aim of ending Lang's dictatorship. Although Heffron was the public face of the opposition to Lang, McKell had the numbers in the parliamentary party. He had kept his head down and worked quietly against Lang from within. McKell had not openly split from Labor, had been an effective member of the Opposition and had quietly been building his reputation and strength. He was a centrist, unlike Heffron who had a more radical background. The prospect of the Labor leadership was personally attractive to McKell, but he also felt a sense of duty to do what he could to rescue the Party from the disastrous position Lang had put it in.

At by-elections in April 1939, Heffron candidates won Hurstville and Waverley in suburban Sydney from the United Australia Party (UAP)/United Country Party (UCP) Coalition Government led by Bertram Stevens — unequivocal proof that Lang's appeal had evaporated. Soon after, Labor's Federal Executive intervened and a unity conference comprising representatives of both parties was held in August. Lang's opponents had a comfortable majority and took control of the State Executive. The unity conference returned to the Parliamentary Labor Party the right to elect its own leader. This automatically meant the end of Lang who was too unpopular with his colleagues to have any chance of success. In the Caucus ballot on 5 September 1939, McKell had 13 votes, Lang 12 and Heffron seven. In the next ballot, all of Heffron's votes went to McKell. Within weeks of the outbreak of the Second World War, McKell was Leader of the Opposition.

One of his successors as Labor Premier, Bob Carr, has described McKell as close to an ideal choice: "A man with a classic background of working-class deprivation, a former manual worker and union official who had qualified in law, an experienced former minister with contacts throughout the administration, skilled in the methods of government - and a farmer to boot".[9]

McKell's approach to returning Labor to office was not dissimilar to Gough Whitlam's tripartite strategy as Opposition Leader: the party, the policy, the people.

A challenge for McKell was to assemble a team of strong candidates that had electoral appeal. The disarray in most of the branches and bitterness remaining after previous faction fights made the chances of the best candidate being endorsed remote. To remedy this situation, the State Executive, in a behind-the-scenes deal, agreed to give McKell the final say in selecting candidates. Some were known to him personally, others were recommended by trusted sources.

Labor branches were told that, owing to the non-availability of records due to changes in administration, it was impossible to check satisfactorily on who was eligible to vote in preselection ballots. The State Executive would interview all candidates and make the selections itself. To placate branch opinion, State Electorate Councils were asked to hold a ballot of those candidates the Executive deemed eligible for selection. The winning candidate's name was then to be forwarded to the Executive. All candidates for selection presented themselves before the Executive in Sydney on the weekend of 18 and 19 January 1941. Officially, they were evaluated by the Executive which then selected the appropriate candidate for the electorate concerned. Unofficially, the candidate endorsed by McKell was successful. The quality of many of the candidates gave Labor a new credibility.

McKell took a particular interest in the selection of rural candidates. New South Wales Labor had traditionally been strong in the country and he realised that there was much potential to win seats, particularly as many rural voters were disillusioned with the Country Party. In 1925, Labor won 16 country electorates; in 1935 it won three.[10] The *Daily Telegraph* commented: "The Labor Party is basing its hopes of success in country electorates largely on the care taken in selecting candidates. Most Labor candidates have an intimate knowledge of country affairs and requirements and many are expected to oust the sitting Country Party members".[11] The *Sydney Morning Herald* described the rural candidates as "practical farmers, shire councillors, stock breeders and men from local families of long standing".[12] Many of those who were elected became major figures in the years to come: George Enticknap, Eddie Graham, Roger Nott, Jack Renshaw, Billy Sheahan.

The defeat of Lang did not bring an end to Labor's internal divisions. Lang and his supporters broke away to form the Australian Labor Party (Non-Communist) on 18 April 1940. By now, they were a rump with little support. This led to negotiations that eventually achieved unity in early 1941. Non-Communist Labor branches amalgamated with the Official Party and all Lang MLAs were re-endorsed.

The Communist Party had been active in the struggle against Lang and thus had a significant presence in the Labor Party. New South Wales Vice-President Jack Hughes and State Secretary Bill Evans were undercover Communists. As a result, in August 1940, the Federal

Executive once again intervened and dissolved the New South Wales Executive. The group of anti-Lang and anti-Communist union officials who took over remained in control of the Party until 1952. This faction was McKell's power base. Its leaders worked hard to rebuild and stabilise the Labor Party. Federally, the group was aligned with Ben Chifley (Treasurer 1941-49, Prime Minister 1945-49), a close friend of McKell. The Communist group formed the State or Hughes-Evans Labor Party. It had some union backing and branch support but no parliamentarians and little electoral popularity. The Hughes-Evans Party merged with the Communist Party in 1943.

Around the same time, a revolt broke out among country branches, spearheaded by disgruntled local members, some with frustrated parliamentary ambitions, and Lang sympathisers. It was fuelled by traditional anti-urban feelings. These disaffected elements formed a breakaway Country Labor Party. Most country branches, however, remained loyal to Official Labor. The rural revolt had little impact on the forthcoming election and minimal long-term significance.[13]

These splinter groups proved to be of no more than nuisance value. By the time of the 1941 election, the majority of branches, unions and parliamentarians were united behind McKell. In a masterstroke, McKell and his allies coined the term Official Labor to legitimise the mainstream party.

During his years as an MLA, McKell had read widely, discussed issues and ideas with his broad network of contacts, and thought deeply about the problems facing New South Wales. He was particularly influenced by United States President Franklin Roosevelt's New Deal conservation initiatives. McKell's main conclusion was that all future development should be guided by the principles of planning and conservation. He characteristically looked for rational solutions based on expert advice. A publication issued by him in 1946 stated that the most significant feature of his government was:

> ... a determination to work on the lines of a master plan. There would be no more bits and pieces reforms dictated by the expediency of the moment. There would be no more jabs and stabs at public works, all disconnected, often over-lapping ... Nor, the Government determined, should there be allowed any further deterioration of the land itself ... All the future development of the State... should be carried through on the basis of scientific planning.[14]

McKell rejuvenated Labor's platform with his wide-ranging master plan of co-ordinated reforms for both city and country.

McKell made a deliberate break with Lang's style. Temperamentally, he could not have emulated it even if he had wanted to. Politically, it was a necessity. McKell refused to indulge in political adventurism and fiery populist rhetoric. His solid, safe, respectable image was an appealing one to an electorate tired of Lang's vituperative extremism. The replacement of Lang deprived the UAP/UCP government of one of its main electoral assets.

Lang had indiscriminately attacked all aspects of the UAP/UCP Government's performance in an aggressive and exaggerated fashion. McKell was more selective in his opposition. He set out subtly to undermine the Government by characterizing it as complacent and inactive, a 'do nothing' administration. It was a fruitful line of attack. During the UAP/UCP Government's term from 1932-41, few major public works were commenced in the Sydney area and there was little of significance in the way of rural development. In the five years to 1939, £46 million was spent on capital works compared to £90 million in 1924-29.[15]

As New South Wales Labor was reunifying, the UAP/UCP Government was fracturing. In the mid-1930s, a rebel group emerged in the party room. Stevens' authoritarian response generated growing resentment. The aggressive and forceful Deputy Premier and Country Party Leader, Michael Bruxner, was a dominant figure in the government. This led to further friction as it was resented by many in the

UAP. The internal unrest culminated in Stevens losing a confidence vote in the Legislative Assembly, moved by a former minister and prominent dissident, Eric Spooner. Alec Mair succeeded him as Premier on 5 August 1939, but the divisions remained.[16]

That McKell was cutting through was shown by a series of by-election results. The UCP lost Barwon in western New South Wales in November 1940. Labor's Roy Hefferen polled 55 per cent of the vote on the final count. In September 1940, the UAP candidate in Croydon, which Stevens had held in 1938 with 69.6 per cent of the primary vote, was forced to preferences, retaining the seat with 56.1 per cent. Even more worrying for the Government was the loss of Ryde later the same month. It was the sort of Sydney suburban seat Labor had to win if it was to gain office. The Labor candidate won the by-election with 50.5 per cent after preferences had been distributed. McKell commented: "Croydon was the first portent; Ryde shows beyond all doubt that public opinion in New South Wales has swung solidly behind the war and domestic policies of the Official Labor Party".[17]

Winning in 1941

Mair argued that, in view of the wartime emergency, Labor should join with the UAP and UCP in a coalition government allowing the postponement of the general election. Scenting victory, McKell unhesitatingly rejected the idea and Mair reluctantly announced that an election would be held on 10 May 1941. Labor faced a big challenge, having won only 30 (including Heffron Labor) of the 90 seats in 1938.

In his policy speech, delivered at Waterloo Town Hall on 21 April, McKell outlined a program that was both bold and far-reaching, yet solidly based and well thought-out. He contrasted this with the UAP/UCP Government's previous lethargy and current procrastination. McKell's message was that New South Wales could be revitalised without jeopardising the war effort in any way. It would, in fact, be improved by Labor's initiatives. There were also promises of reforms in areas of traditional concern to Labor such as health, housing, education and industrial matters. The icing on the cake was a pledge to abolish the unpopular unemployment relief tax on wages.[18]

McKell unveiled a detailed program for the rehabilitation of country New South Wales in his rural policy speech, delivered at West Wyalong on 23 April. Country dwellers were promised improvements in water and soil conservation, closer settlement and marketing. The debts of the past would be wiped out and a new era of prosperity ushered in based on conservation and planned development.[19]

Mair delivered his policy speech in his electorate of Albury on 22 April. It was strong on patriotism and reminders of what had happened to the state under Lang. Mair accused the Labor Party of forcing an election at a time when unity was vital by refusing to join a coalition government. He catalogued improvements that had occurred since the UAP/UCP took office at the height of the Depression – unsurprisingly to his advantage – and promised wide-ranging improvements, although only after the war had been won.[20]

Bruxner gave his policy speech on 24 April. He reiterated many of Mair's points but with "a rural emphasis and with a bite that the gentler Mair would have found hard to carry off". Bruxner said that the war was all important, "and winning it the first consideration; that McKell was bringing party politics into the election was almost treasonable and certainly prejudicial to the war effort".[21]

The battlelines, then, were clearly drawn. Labor, in the belief that the electorate was fed up with the Mair Government's conservative approach and was ready for change, promised renewed vigour in the war effort, reduced taxation and a wide-ranging program of social and rural reform. The Mair Government, on the other hand, based its appeal on the belief that in a time of crisis the electors would stick with an administration they knew rather than allowing an untried Labor team into power, especially in view of the disastrous end of the last Labor government under Lang.

The respective leaders' approaches are neatly summarised by an exchange in the press between Mair and McKell. Mair stated that he believed the government would be returned because in a time of crisis the people would be reluctant to "change horses in mid-stream".[22] McKell responded: "If the horse is broken-winded, spavined and never had been good for a hard gallop at any rate, to refuse to change when a good animal is available is not only pitiful but rank lunacy".[23]

The result was a resounding victory for McKell, with Labor winning 54 of the 90 seats in the Legislative Assembly. The UAP was reduced from the 34 it held before the election to 14 and the UCP from 21 to 12. McKell's rural strategy paid off, with the number of country seats held by Labor increasing from three to 14. Two more were won at the 1944 election and the total peaked at 17 after Labor won Albury at a by-election in November 1946.[24]

An unusually high total of ten Independents was elected, most of them disgruntled former UAP supporters. The total UAP vote was 20.3 per cent. Independent UAP candidates polled 3.3 per cent. If the UCP's vote of 11.1 per cent is added to the official UAP vote, the total for the Coalition was 31.4 per cent compared to Labor's

50.8 per cent. The Hughes-Evans Party received 5.6 per cent of the vote. In two-party preferred terms, the Labor vote has been estimated as 57 per cent (although with the large number of Independent candidates such a calculation should be treated with some caution).

For a government that had never been particularly active to espouse a policy of deliberate inactivity, for whatever reason, was a misreading of the mood of the electorate. Attempts to resuscitate memories of Lang and to invoke the seriousness of the war situation were not enough to save it. The attempt to exploit the war for political purposes may have provoked a backlash of resentment. Bruxner's dominant role in the government was a double liability, in that it was resented by city voters, and felt by country voters to be proof that the UCP had neglected them.

Reunited and with an attractive new leader, Labor had fresh credibility. The electorate, leaving one crisis — the Depression — behind, and not yet feeling the full impact of the next one — Japan had not yet entered the War — was hungry for progress and improvement. McKell was able to respond to this mood by aggressively carrying the message to the voters that Labor had the personnel and policies to take New South Wales through its present troubles and into the future.

McKell as Premier

The *Sydney Morning Herald* commented that the Premier had "always adopted a common-sense, moderate view in politics and, while always a hard hitter, has never embraced extremist philosophies. The glamour of the position leaves him cold. He prefers the simple tastes and pursuits of the people".[25] The *Daily Telegraph* described McKell as "a middle-sized man. Though compactly, rather than strongly, built, his shoulders and arms recall his boilermaking days. He would have made a good axeman if he had been caught young. He has straightforward features. He has a good broad forehead".[26]

In office, McKell was determined to deliver. The minutes of his first Cabinet meeting record: "Ministers to see that Under-Secretaries are supplied with copies of Labor's Policy Speech and given to understand that matters contained therein are to be put into operation ... Premier urged Ministers to get busy on preparation of bills in accordance with Labor's Policy".[27] The Premier asked his ministers for regular updates on their implementation of his election platform.

Caution, rationality, and pragmatism were the hallmarks of McKell's approach to government. He preferred damage avoidance to damage control. There was a deliberate attempt to minimise risk-taking and anticipate and deal with potential problems by careful planning. As little as possible was left to chance and decisions were made only after taking the best advice available and with a solid grasp of facts. Also prominent was a preference for compromise rather than confrontation, and the use of negotiation to bridge differences.

McKell's main concern was to establish and maintain a stable and responsible style of government. He strove to project an image of unity and competence. It was important to convince the electorate that the Labor Party could govern in this manner, particularly after the turbulent history of preceding Labor governments. By adopting a pragmatic political style, McKell aimed to consolidate Labor in power and implement as much of his election platform as possible. He was in for the long haul.

Aware of the need to preserve his political capital, McKell concentrated on what was realistically achievable. Controversial issues were sometimes avoided, and plans dropped or modified rather than arouse virulent opposition:

> Late in 1942 Prime Minister John Curtin reintroduced the uniquely dangerous issue of conscription. McKell took no direct stand, refusing Opposition attempts to have the issue discussed in the Assembly. He avoided the issue when later addressing the 1943 New South Wales Annual Conference. Many other issues

were put on hold or watered down. With Labor
doing so well in country electorates, the promise
to introduce electoral reform based on one-vote,
one-value lacked priority. *A Greater Sydney Bill*,
promised in July 1941, was not proceeded with,
in the face of certain confrontation. Labor's 1941
Annual Conference was promised compulsory
unionism; after a storm of opposition, what
was finally introduced two years later was a
provision that awards might include preference
to unionists.[28]

There were, however, occasions on which McKell did
not hesitate to take a tough, uncompromising stand. As
a firm believer in states' rights, McKell found himself
in conflict with his Federal colleagues Prime Minister
John Curtin and Treasurer Ben Chifley over their
1942 plan to take over the states' income tax powers.
He responded that he could not accept the proposed
changes as this would be a betrayal of the trust the
people had placed in his government. The power to
tax was the power to govern. McKell added that he
appreciated the exigencies of war but also appreciated
the fact that there was a constitutional system
that would continue to operate after the war. He
presciently predicted that the uniform tax proposals,
if accepted, would inevitably become a permanent part
of the Australian political system.[29]

On the eve of the 1942 New South Wales Annual
Conference, McKell announced that he was joining

the other premiers in a High Court challenge to the Commonwealth's action. It proved to be a serious political misjudgement as Curtin and Chifley had the numbers in the Labor Party. The Conference, despite strong opposition from McKell, proceeded to endorse overwhelmingly the uniform tax proposal. He subsequently withdrew from the High Court action. McKell's strong convictions about the future of federalism prevailed over his usual political caution.[30]

McKell set up a powerful political and administrative machine that was to play a large part in maintaining Labor in power for the next 24 years. One of his main concerns was to ensure that his knowledge of and control over his government was as complete as possible.

The Premier's chief bureaucratic adviser was the powerful Chairman of the Public Service Board, Wallace Wurth. Always an excellent judge of character and ability, McKell in the 1920s had recognised Wurth's potential and fostered his career. As well as providing "shrewd counsel and advice",[31] Wurth was an invaluable source of inside information which meant that McKell sometimes knew about developments in departments before the relevant minister.

McKell monitored the performance of his ministers closely. His first Cabinet had a nucleus of capable performers — Bob Heffron, Clarrie Martin, Joe Cahill,

Reg Downing — but others were mediocrities or past their best. Education Minister Clive Evatt (younger brother of HV Evatt) was an incorrigible schemer and troublemaker. McKell saw himself as "a tough, driving leader" who needed to "rule with a strong hand".[32] He made it clear that incompetence and impropriety would not be tolerated.

McKell insisted that all submissions for Cabinet be circulated well in advance and, with the assistance of Wurth, evaluated them carefully. The Budget Branch of Treasury, which McKell had strengthened by the appointment of a group of talented public servants, carefully scrutinised the financial aspects of Cabinet submissions. As a result, the Premier sometimes knew more about the submission than the minister proposing it.

Although he co-ordinated and drove the overall agenda, McKell expected ministers to perform and did not interfere in their portfolios needlessly. When the inexperienced Minister of Justice Reg Downing listed some matters relating to release of prisoners for Cabinet consideration, McKell told him to make his own decisions and not hide behind Cabinet.[33]

McKell was keenly aware of the importance to the government of good relations with the Labor machine and the trade unions. Downing, a protégé who had been an MLC since 1940, was put in charge of liaison with the New South Wales Executive and the Labor Council. The influential Bob King, Secretary of the Labor Council 1934-58, was a key contact. Downing had a lengthy trade union background and was the latest recruit to the Government from the Trades Hall. He was a key member of the faction that had taken control of the New South Wales branch after the removal of the Langites and the Hughes-Evans group. In addition to his wide network of contacts in the unions and labour movement, Downing possessed abilities of a high order as a conciliator, negotiator, and trouble-shooter. Every week, senior Labor officials met with Downing to discuss problems that had arisen and sort out difficulties. Downing was also a useful intermediary and buffer when McKell was faced with unacceptable requests from the labour movement. McKell's other means of placating the extra-parliamentary party was by delivering a solid program of social and industrial reform.[34]

Thanks to McKell's efforts, the internecine conflict between the parliamentary and extra-parliamentary parties that had hampered or destroyed all previous New South Wales Labor governments was noticeably absent between 1941-47.

McKell faced the onerous challenge of total war. A vigorous civil defence and air raid precaution program (known as National Emergency Services) was driven by Bob Heffron. McKell set up a War Effort Co-ordination Committee chaired by himself. Much of Australia's industrial and construction capacity was in New South Wales and the Premier made sure it was mobilised to the full. The New South Wales Government was responsible for:

> ... 800 defence projects, including 40 aerodromes in Australia and nearby islands. Other projects included the building of gun emplacements, pipelines, storage depots, wharves, military camps. The Walsh Island shipbuilding yard was recommissioned; its floating dock was in service by January 1942, enabling repairs to 63 ships in the next four years. The New South Wales Department of Main Roads became the construction authority for North Queensland strategic roads, at one stage building 402 miles in less than half a year. Early in 1943, almost half of Australia's munitions factories were in New South Wales most decentralised for strategic reasons outside Sydney or on its fringes, for example at Villawood and St. Mary's.[35]

Parliament

In Parliament, McKell's personal style was factual, straightforward and lacking in flamboyance. He preferred civility and conciliation to aggressive confrontation. McKell was, however, a formidable opponent, capable of delivering a detailed, fact-studded onslaught when the occasion demanded.[36]

An example of McKell's decency in dealing with his fellow MLAs, and his decency in general, is given in this speech by UAP MLA Joseph Jackson in April 1944:

> The late Julian Ashton painted two replicas of the portrait [of Sir Henry Parkes] in the National Gallery, one copy of which is in the Commonwealth Parliamentary Gallery, and I was asked by Julian Ashton if I could buy or secure a purchaser for the other. It was beyond my reach but I thought that the Premier might feel disposed to make the purchase on behalf of the State, and I suggested that course to him ... The Premier said he would consider what I had had to say, and whether he should make the purchase on behalf of the Government. He informed me a few days later that he could not do that, but that he would effect that purchase from his private purse, and make the presentation to the house in appreciation of his accession to the office of Premier of this State. I want to say that I regard that as a great benefaction to this house and to every member of it, and I should be lacking in my sense of duty if I did not place on record these facts in relation to what I regard as the finest and most generous gesture I have seen in my 22 years' experience in this house, and also the nicest. That is my tribute, and one that I think is due to the Premier in the closing session of this Parliament.
>
> Mr. McKELL: I desire to express to the member for Nepean my thanks for his very generous, and,

I might say, unexpected remarks. I should like to inform members that the reason the portrait of Sir Henry Parkes hangs in this Chamber today is not solely because of something that I did, but because of the thoughtfulness of the member for Nepean in bringing all the facts under my notice. Mr. JACKSON: You found the money! Mr. McKELL: I am very happy indeed to be associated in any way with this magnificent portrait and - if I might humbly say so - to have my name associated in any way with that of the great man who sat for it. I am happy, too, for another reason because it brought contentment, happiness and peace to a great Australian in his last hours. It was the lifelong wish of Julian Ashton that this portrait should hang in the Legislative Assembly chamber of New South Wales. A similar portrait is in the National Art Gallery, and there is one in the Federal House of Parliament at Canberra. Everyone who was present when the painting was unveiled in its present spot was delighted at the expressions of the artist, whom we were happy to have with us on that occasion. It was delightful to see the happiness on his face, and as we all knew that his hours with us could be but few, we were intensely gratified with him in the fulfilment of his lifelong wish that his painting should hang in this chamber. We felt that his few remaining hours would be so much the more peaceful and contented and so much the happier. The little act for which I was responsible was something that gave me very great pleasure.[37]

McKell respected and admired the institution of

parliament. On one occasion he told the House: "It is the duty of every one of us to make this an institution of respect and reverence in the eyes of the people of the State".[38] At the end of 1943 McKell commented "in the time of greatest crisis this House returned to first principles. We went back to the principles upon which our democratic institutions are based. These principles involve the absolute, the complete and the unfettered freedom of the representatives of the people to express themselves as fully as they think fit".[39]

McKell attempted to make Parliament work effectively rather than to dominate it: "I have been long enough in the House to realise, and I am sufficiently old-fashioned enough to believe, that the interests of the nation are better served by unrestricted rather than restricted debate".[40] The gag and guillotine were not applied during McKell's term of office and time for debate, both on legislation and on private members' business, was maximised.

On the last sitting day before Parliament was dissolved for the 1944 election McKell said:

> We have seen in this chamber during the last three years democracy working in its purest and finest form. Every one of the ninety Members of this House has had a full and free opportunity to express himself. This is a great achievement. I have sat in many Parliaments here but this is the first within my knowledge in which every

Member of the House has been unrestricted in debate.[41]

Lack of a majority in the Legislative Council, where Labor had 22 MLCs compared to the Coalition's 37, was a serious obstacle. The McKell Government was defeated 107 times in divisions in the Council in less than six years while its Coalition predecessor had been defeated only 24 times in seven and a half years.[42]

Reg Downing was McKell's surprise choice as Leader of the Government in the upper house. McKell told Downing to keep proceedings, as far as possible, on a rational level and to avoid provoking the Opposition unnecessarily. Downing's reasonableness quickly won him the respect of many leading Opposition MLCs, including Sir Henry Manning who acted as Leader of the Opposition without ever formally assuming the title. After Manning retired in 1958 he wrote to Downing: "I would like you to know how grateful I am to you personally for the attitude you always adopted about any of the suggestions I may have made. It is that sort of attitude which makes for ultimate success and makes discussion of difficult matters worthwhile".[43] Undoubtedly, there was confrontation and obstruction, but Downing, with McKell's support, was often able to negotiate the passage of important legislation through the upper house, though sometimes in a truncated form.[44]

In conformity with his 1941 election pledge, McKell attempted to reform, then abolish the Council. Ken Turner has summed up what happened:

> In November 1943 McKell produced a bill, supposedly a first step towards abolition, providing for direct election of the Council and weakening of its powers over finance. It was defeated in the Council. In December 1946, a surprise abolition attempt was defeated in the Council, only by the casting vote of the President. Although neither was an all-out attack, pushed to a referendum to break the deadlock, they were not merely ritualistic. They were partly a gesture to reassure the Party faithful and to press home the blame for delays in promised actions. Perhaps they were also hints to Legislative Councillors that it might be discreet not to be seen as obstructive. There were also good pragmatic reasons not to press the attack further. In the wartime context of 1943, a Labor Government had better things to do than be distracted by lengthy deadlock procedures.[45]

1944 triumph

McKell based his appeal for the 27 May 1944 election on "the solid foundation of promises kept, on the unchallenged record of three years of unremitting work, devotion to the war effort, and enlightened legislative and administrative action".[46] In his policy speech he summarised in detail the Government's record in promoting the war effort and in the social, industrial and rural areas. McKell then went on to outline his plans for the postwar world with promises of improvements in housing, social welfare, health, education and working conditions.[47]

McKell attempted to defuse the backlash against the Federal Labor Government's use of its war powers to regulate many areas by admitting that criticism was "to some extent well-based". He promised that his government would, if re-elected, legislate to ensure that all regulations were valid for a limited period only, after which they would be reviewed by parliament. He also pointed to the non-use of the gag in parliament as proof of his government's commitment to fundamental democratic values.[48]

Reg Weaver had succeeded Mair as Leader of the State Opposition in February 1944. There was a feeling amongst his colleagues that the affable Mair lacked the toughness and drive needed to give the Opposition some sort of chance in the coming election. Weaver certainly was aggressive, but this was combined with an arrogance and instability of temperament. In his earlier career as a minister (1929-30, 1932-35), Weaver had succeeded in antagonising the labour movement, the Graziers' Association, the Protestant Churches and the British Medical Association.[49]

In his policy speech, Weaver made great play of charges that the McKell Government had stood idly by "while regimentation and rule by regulation had run mad".[50] This was, he claimed, part of a plan "which Labor governments have already worked out" for "complete socialisation".[51] The Leader of the Opposition also had plans for a better postwar world, in some respects not dissimilar to McKell's. Weaver said that his party believed "every citizen should have the right of continuous employment, and that each individual should have economic security of the highest standard, that will enable him to purchase a home of his own and attain improved social conditions and amenities to the full capacity of the State".[52]

By 1944, the State Opposition was in complete disarray. The UAP had disintegrated, amidst bitter recriminations, under the stress of defeat in the 1941 state and the 1943 federal elections. In November 1943, the main remnant became the Democratic Party and all State parliamentarians joined the new grouping. However, an influential breakaway group, the Liberal Democratic Party, refused to join the new conservative party and endorsed its own candidates for the 1944 election. Relations with the Country Party also broke down and no electoral agreement was able to be negotiated between the two major Opposition parties.

McKell's approach to government was triumphantly

vindicated by the 1944 result. Labor won 56 seats, two more than in 1941. Most Labor MLAs greatly increased their majorities, particularly in rural areas. Lang had been expelled in 1943 after a campaign of persistent disruption and had once more formed a breakaway party. By now, he had little support and his group won only his seat of Auburn plus Newtown. The Democratic Party could muster only 12 seats and the Country Party ten. There were ten Independents. The combined Labor and Lang Labor primary vote was 54.5 per cent (Labor 45.2 per cent, Lang 9.3 per cent) compared to the Democratic, Liberal Democratic and Country Party total of 33.2 per cent (Democratic 18.9 per cent, Liberal Democratic 3.9 per cent, Country 10.4 per cent). Labor's two-party preferred result has been calculated as 59 per cent. McKell became the first New South Wales Labor premier to serve a second consecutive term. On 26 March 1945, he broke Lang's record as the longest serving New South Wales Labor premier.

Second term

With the Government re-elected and the end of the war in sight, McKell's attention turned increasingly to postwar reconstruction. He outlined his vision for the future in a speech in January 1947. It reflected McKell's belief that the role of government was to liberate not dominate the individual. His theme was that the state was not an abstract body which could be organised and directed without regard to the people in it:

> To improve the state we must improve conditions for the people living in it. We must improve the people's surroundings, professional and economic opportunities, education and cultural outlook. The Government believes that all people have the right to the best education and modern amenities, whether they live in remote country districts or the heart of Sydney. We want to improve the welfare of the individual, and consequently the welfare of the state. The Government needs the co-operation of the people, just as the people need guidance by the state administration. National problems can only be worked out by a joint effort.[53]

McKell hoped to create an egalitarian society based on planning, conservation, scientific progress, and rational decision-making. Some of this would now be characterised as a rather naïve belief in the "perfectibility of man". It is also suggestive of the exaggerated respect of the autodidact for experts. However, such ideas were very much in tune with contemporary currents in society. There was a widespread belief in the creation of a new and better world.

McKell's postwar vision had much in common with that of Prime Minister Ben Chifley and they worked closely together on projects such as the Snowy Mountains

Scheme. However, McKell did not hesitate to distance himself publicly from the Federal Government when he disagreed with its actions. As Vince Kelly wrote in his biography of McKell:

> [He] firmly believed that the states would continue to exist, and while they existed their sovereign rights should be preserved. It went deeper than that with him. He had worked hard for the enormous advances made by New South Wales during the war and for its postwar development. His wartime experiences had caused him to distrust much of Canberra's thinking and its bureaucratic approach.[54]

In 1946, when Chifley, armed with a High Court decision, proposed to make the existing uniform tax system permanent, McKell was outspoken in his opposition. At that year's Premiers' Conference, speaking on behalf of all the premiers, he observed:

> The essence of true responsibility in government is that there should be some direct and substantial degree of relationship between the government expending the money and the taxpayer bearing the burden of taxation ... It is my sincere belief that if one legislative body, supreme in its own field, were made financially and therefore generally dependent upon another, there would not only be an endless series of difficulties in the adjustment of Commonwealth-State relations, but we would have but a mockery of a true system of federal government.[55]

Although he was unsuccessful, McKell emerged from the Premiers' Conference with enhanced prestige as the acknowledged leader of the states. Even the normally, by this time, hostile Sydney press praised his stand against the Commonwealth.

McKell's desire to implement his visionary schemes came up against some harsh political realities. A major problem was widespread postwar industrial disruption as unions battled for their share of the fruits of victory. McKell did what he could to deal with a complex and intractable situation. He tried to become as publicly and actively involved as possible in solving disputes in the hope of convincing the voters that everything feasible was being done to deal with a situation that admitted of no easy solution. A subsidiary aim was to persuade the electorate that Labor, with its links to the union movement, was more competent and better placed to deal with industrial unrest than the Opposition.

Another central policy was unwavering support for the principles of arbitration as the best means of resolving disputes and as a bulwark against industrial anarchy. McKell also strongly attacked Communist influence in the union movement and called on militant union leaders to show a sense of responsibility by minimising stoppages. Finally, McKell was also prepared to give some concessions to ease the industrial pressure. The main example was an extra week of annual leave, a key union demand, which McKell legislated for in 1944.

The McKell Government was undoubtedly damaged by the major inconvenience the tsunami of strikes inflicted on ordinary people. The Opposition and Sydney press exploited the situation, claiming the industrial unrest was a Communist-inspired attempt to undermine democracy. However, McKell's strategy of projecting an image of the Government working together with reasonable elements in the union movement to minimise strikes was an effective one. His measured, firm but reasonable, stance resonated. While the voters were not happy, they were not convinced that anyone else would be able to handle the situation more effectively.

A major achievement of McKell's second term was his successful struggle to appoint the first Australian-born New South Wales Governor. When Lord Wakehurst concluded his term, McKell proposed Captain John Armstrong of the Royal Australian Navy as his successor. The British Government was strongly opposed to the appointment of an Australian and responded by proposing the King's brother-in-law, Michael Bowes-Lyon. McKell refused to be intimidated, bluntly rejecting Bowes-Lyon and countering with Australian General John Northcott, who was the designated Commander of the British

Commonwealth Occupation Force in Japan. The British reluctantly backed off and Northcott became Governor on 1 August 1946.[56]

Chris Cunneen has commented:

> By deciding on a distinguished Australian military officer with service in the recent war, and no political connections, [McKell] had effectively precluded any criticism. Bowes-Lyon's nomination had been an inept attempt to link the royal family to the governorship and the suggestion attracted little enthusiasm in New South Wales, especially when compared to an Australian-born General. In the area of symbolic sovereignty at least, the government of New South Wales had asserted its independence from the British Dominions Office.[57]

Caucus problems

McKell had to deal with an increasingly strong rebel group in Caucus in his second term. After the landslide 1941 victory, his authority had been largely unquestioned. Nonetheless, two Labor lawyers, Education Minister Clive Evatt and backbencher Abe Landa, soon emerged as malcontents.

After the 1944 election, McKell faced a less acquiescent party room. Ambitious backbenchers were restless and frustrated over their failure to become ministers. McKell made a tactical error in choosing to confront them rather than neutralising the more capable by promoting them. Cabinet needed renewal and several of the rebels became senior figures in succeeding ALP Governments. A few unreconstructed "Langsters" still had scores to settle. These dissident elements were only too happy to join Evatt and Landa in harassing the Premier. This led to a restiveness in Caucus that had a disproportionate effect on McKell, who was wounded by what he saw as ingratitude for all that he had done.

An early sign of trouble was the narrow re-election of Clive Evatt to Cabinet despite McKell's clearly expressed wish that he be dropped. The Premier responded by refusing to give Evatt a portfolio. He was made an Assistant Minister and demoted to second-last in Cabinet seniority. This move served only to exacerbate the problem, as it was resented by many of the 29 MLAs who had voted for Evatt.

Further difficulties emerged in July 1944. The exclusion of the Labor MLA for the area, Jack Seiffert, from the Kosciusko Park Trust led to criticism of the Premier in Caucus. McKell had little personal regard for Seiffert and had appointed Garfield Barwick and NL Roberts, both of whom he regarded as dedicated conservationists, to the Trust. Billy Sheahan, supported by Evatt, moved that any future appointments to such trusts or public bodies should be considered by a Caucus sub-committee in consultation with Cabinet.

McKell responded by declaring that he regarded such a motion as one of no-confidence. After heated debate, a compromise motion, that ministers should in future consult with the relevant local member over appointments to trusts and other similar bodies, was carried unanimously.

Another confrontation occurred in October 1945 on McKell's return from an overseas trip. Two backbenchers moved for the appointment of four assistant ministers to Cabinet. McKell, who was infuriated by what he regarded as a carefully orchestrated plot hatched in his absence, told Caucus that he would resign if the motion was carried. The proposal did not proceed.

There was unrest in Caucus over McKell's alleged slowness to deal with abuses in the liquor trade, the implication being that the Premier was beholden to the powerful brewery interests. McKell did, in fact, bring down liquor reform legislation in 1946. It provided for a referendum (subsequently lost) on the contentious hours of opening question.

Abe Landa, supported by the rebel group, pursued a long-running campaign in Caucus for legislation to ban the reporting of divorce proceedings in the press, particularly the lurid accounts regularly appearing in the Sunday newspapers. McKell compromised by passing legislation in 1946 to make it an offence to publish reports of judicial proceedings that would "tend to encourage depravity, or would tend to injure the morals of the public".[58] Landa claimed that McKell had caved in to pressure from newspaper proprietors.

McKell suffered a serious defeat in Caucus in February 1946 over plans to continue the zoning system for bread, milk and ice. Under Commonwealth National Security Regulations, the delivery of these commodities in wartime was confined to a single distributor in zones or blocks into which Sydney, Newcastle and other centres had been divided. When the Commonwealth regulations expired, McKell, feeling that it was premature to jettison these controls, proposed the State government continue them. There was, however, concern in Caucus that zoning was unpopular amongst women voters as it had allegedly led to rationing, short supplies and inferior goods. The Housewives' Association and Labor Women's Conference both condemned the zoning system. The rebels seized on the issue and managed to rebuff McKell by pushing through Caucus a resolution for an immediate end to zoning.

McKell was temperamentally unable to shrug off criticism he regarded as unfair. As he became more obsessed with his plans for postwar reconstruction, he became less tolerant of differing opinions. He also lost some of the people skills that had served him so well earlier in his career, seeing himself as the prophet who knew best. As well, McKell was physically and emotionally exhausted by his enormous workload, the demands of the war, implementing his agenda and dealing with incessant political problems. McKell had been convinced at the height of the conflict in the Pacific that a Japanese invasion of Australia was imminent. The burden of wartime leadership had undermined his once robust health. In particular, he suffered from chronic insomnia.

On 13 February 1946, McKell announced that he was retiring before the next election. His supporters in the Party Executive, Cabinet and Caucus responded by organising votes of confidence in his leadership and urging him to reconsider his decision. In response, it became increasingly apparent that McKell was relenting and would stay on. Then came Chifley's offer of the Governor-Generalship.

The process leading to McKell's appointment was not as straightforward as it seemed at the time. At one stage, Chifley had considered appointing Lord Mountbatten but he was not interested. According to John Waugh, who has provided a detailed reconstruction of McKell's appointment:

> Once Chifley had secured cabinet endorsement
> – a careful, but not essential, step – he was able
> to stick to his decision despite opposition from
> his party, the public, the British Government
> and the King. The incident remains a minor

landmark of Australian nationalism, but it is also a reminder of how gradually Australia disengaged from the United Kingdom in the twentieth century. The involvement of the British Government shows that its removal from the process of choosing a Governor-General took time to become complete. Chifley's apparent ambivalence about appointing an Australian to the position hints that his nationalism, and the appointment process, were more complex than the simple fact of McKell's nomination might suggest.[59]

McKell resigned as Premier on 6 February 1947 to take up his viceregal duties.

A *Sydney Morning Herald* editorial commented that McKell's record in office had "followed strictly the lines of modest performance rather than spectacular adventuring. Perhaps he saw enough of political fireworks in his Langist days . . . Safety first and all the time has been the guiding principle of the McKell regime".[60] The editorialist added: "The Labor Party owes him much ... Under his leadership it was rebuilt when misrule and division had laid it virtually in ruins ... His moderation has been an asset to it in the constituencies. He restored popular confidence in Labor's ability to govern when that confidence seemed to have been destroyed".[61] Attorney-General Clarrie Martin expressed regret at McKell's departure in his diary, describing him as "easily the best-informed man in the Party and by far the most experienced administrator".[62]

The struggle for the succession resulted in a slap in the face for McKell. The obvious successor, backed by McKell, was Bob Heffron, an outstanding minister and experienced politician. However, McKell's enemies, determined to inflict one last insult, persuaded Housing Minister Jim McGirr to run. It was a shrewd choice, as, although McGirr was a figure of the second rank, he was popular in Caucus. Reg Downing was the numbers man for Heffron. The contest looked increasingly tight and McKell, in a sign that he had lost his once sure political touch, decided to vote although he had accepted the Governor-Generalship. Downing strongly advised him not to, warning that it would be seen as improper by many MLAs and would give some waverers an excuse to switch to McGirr. McKell persisted and McGirr was victorious on 6 February 1947 by two votes. He proved to be a disastrous Premier.[63]

The legacy

McKell left an imposing legacy. Achievements in the industrial and social area included: the establishment of the State Dockyard at Newcastle; pensions for coal miners; the Joint Coal Board (a Commonwealth-State initiative that greatly improved working conditions for miners); stronger occupational health and safety provisions; the re-establishment of the Government Insurance Office as a provider of affordable general insurance; compulsory third party motor vehicle insurance; major improvements to workers' compensation; increased legal aid; protection of consumers from exploitation by money-lenders; elimination of abuses in the hire-purchase and lay-by systems; an extra week of paid annual leave for all employees; the creation of the Housing Commission to make affordable housing widely available; a second university modelled on the Massachusetts Institute of Technology, the University of New South Wales.

Rural New South Wales benefitted from McKell's initiatives: the *Agricultural Holdings Act* of 1941 placed tenant and share farming on a more secure basis; amendments to the *Farmers' Relief Act* in 1941 significantly assisted in relieving debt; more land was made available for settlement in western New South Wales; 6,000 small farmers were able to reduce their indebtedness by converting from freehold to lease in perpetuity; the accumulated debts of Crown tenants were waived; the *Electricity Development Act* of 1945 brought power to much of rural New South Wales.

One of McKell's first priorities on assuming office was planning for postwar reconstruction. It was essential to assure those in the services and the civilian population that their sacrifices would result in a better world. A Reconstruction Advisory Committee was set up in 1941 to prepare postwar plans. In 1943, this became the Reconstruction and Development Division of the Premier's Department. This Division, assisted by numerous expert committees, was charged with drawing up the blueprints for the future development of New South Wales. In 1946, McKell set up a State Development Council, chaired by himself and consisting of five other ministers, to co-ordinate and oversee the State's postwar development and public works programs.

An important part of this planning was regionalism and decentralisation. A Regional Boundaries Committee was established in 1943 to survey the State and divide it into regions. Regional Development Committees were then set up to develop the resources of their local areas. Government departments were told to use these regional divisions as administrative units.

Conservation of soil, water and forests was an integral part of the McKell agenda. Not long after assuming office, he ordered a state-wide survey of soil erosion problems. This was followed by a comprehensive program of anti-erosion measures. There was, as well, a master plan for water conservation involving the construction of major dams in all areas of the State. A Department of Conservation was created following the

1944 election, and in 1947 the Conservation Authority was set up to co-ordinate the Government's various activities in this field (it became a statutory authority in 1949).

Urban planning received attention. The *Local Government (Town and Country Planning) Act* of 1945 provided for a pioneering town planning scheme which embraced 67 councils and shires in and around the Sydney area. Provision was also made for other local government bodies to prepare similar plans.

Unfortunately, many of McKell's conservation, planning and decentralisation schemes failed to live up to their early promise. This was due more to lack of political support from his successors, who did not share his vision, than to any fault on his part. In the development-obsessed 1950s, planning and the environment had a low priority.[64]

McKell's legacy is substantial and enduring. It is particularly impressive as he was facing the challenges of war and its aftermath.

The Governor-Generalship

McKell's appointment as Governor-General made a significant statement of national identity as he was only the second Australian to hold the office after Isaac Isaacs (1931-36). However, it was vehemently attacked by conservative politicians and newspapers. One of the main critics was Federal Opposition Leader Bob Menzies who, ironically, extended McKell's term and became a friend in later life.

The main overt criticism was that a recently active politician could not be relied upon to act impartially. Behind the scenes there was an element of snobbishness. High Court Judge and later Chief Justice, Sir Owen Dixon, unsuccessfully opposed McKell being granted membership of the Melbourne Club, which was customarily extended to the Governor-General, as he was "horrified at some day having to shake hands with McKell".[65]

Some in the Labor Party were also critical of McKell for becoming the King's representative - feelings that intensified when McKell accepted a knighthood (GCMG) in November 1951. Reg Downing disapproved of McKell's decision and it was the end of their friendship.

McKell was destined to have a controversial term. In 1950-51, the Labor-controlled Senate twice disagreed with the House of Representatives over the *Commonwealth Bank Bill*. As a result, Liberal Prime Minister Menzies asked the Governor-General for a double dissolution. The Opposition claimed that the constitutional requirements had not been met. Menzies provided powerful supporting advice from the Solicitor-General and highly respected constitutional expert, Sir Robert Garran. After careful consideration, McKell decided that Menzies' request was constitutionally valid and he had no option but to grant it. The Menzies Government won a majority in both houses at the April 1951 election.[66]

This entirely proper action was to blight McKell's later years. Some in the Labor Party never forgave him, claiming McKell had betrayed his party and old comrades and "ambushed" Chifley. These charges are unfounded. Reg Downing had bought a property at Goulburn from McKell which meant that they were neighbours. At the height of the crisis, Downing noticed the Governor-General lingering near the boundary fence. Downing sauntered down and the two had a conversation. After the usual pleasantries, McKell said: "I've been talking to Cahalan". "Ned" Cahalan was the New South Wales Parliamentary Draftsman from 1935-53. He was an old friend of McKell's, who often relied on him for legal advice, particularly on sensitive matters. Downing, who also knew Cahalan well, had no doubt what his advice would be in this situation. It was a subtly coded message that McKell was going to grant the double dissolution which was passed on to Chifley.[67]

Chris Cunneen has provided a judicious summation of McKell's viceregal term:

> McKell had undertaken the social duties of his office with zeal and success. He had fully vindicated Chifley's choice of him to democratise the office. Thereafter, Australians could be appointed to represent the Crown with a positive precedent. An ordinary Australian, one who had known the trials of manual labour and poverty and hard labour, one who had had grease under his fingernails, had become the highest embodiment of the Australian people.[68]

In May 1953, McKell left office and retired to his farm at Goulburn.

Epilogue

In 1956, Menzies nominated McKell as the Australian representative on a five member British-appointed Commission under Lord Reid to draw up a constitution for an independent Malaya. McKell's political and governmental experience and inter-personal skills played a significant part in the successful drafting of a document that saw Malaya gain independence and guided it through the important early years.[69]

In later life, McKell faded almost entirely from public view. Living quietly in an apartment in Sydney's eastern suburbs, he spent his time playing bowls, going to the races and keeping up with old friends. A long time Trustee and former Chairman of the Sydney Cricket Ground, McKell was a regular at matches. He was a director of a number of companies.

McKell was largely forgotten by the ALP which paid more attention to the myth of Lang. The neglect of his achievements cast a shadow over McKell's old age. All this began to change in the 1970s. A new generation of Labor activists – Bob Carr, Michael and Shane Easson and John McCarthy - rediscovered McKell and promoted his legacy. Neville Wran named a new State office building after him. There was renewed academic interest in McKell, culminating in Chris Cunneen's authoritative biography. All of this brought comfort to his final years. McKell died on 11 January 1985, aged 93. Lady McKell survived him by six months.

The modern world has grown blasé about "from boilermaker to Governor-General" stories. This should not be allowed to devalue McKell's achievements. Through determination and ability, he overcame disadvantage to achieve outstanding success, both personally and politically. McKell's environmental vision now seems particularly far-sighted. The people of New South Wales were fortunate to have him at the helm to steer the State through the critical war years and the challenging transition to peace. In 1941, it was a case of "cometh the hour, cometh the man".

Notes

1   This section draws on the definitive account of McKell's early years, Chris Cunneen, *William John McKell: Boilermaker, Premier, Governor-General*, UNSW Press, Sydney, 2000.

2   Cunneen, *William John McKell: Boilermaker, Premier, Governor-General*, p. 13.

3   The bout was described in a profile in the *Sun*, 10 May 1944.

4   See Robin Archer, Joy Damousi, Murray Goot and Sean Scalmer, (eds), *The Conscription Conflict and the Great War*, Monash University Publishing, Melbourne, 2016.

5   *Daily Telegraph*, 3 June 1944.

6   *Sydney Morning Herald*, 15 April 1941.

7   Terry Irving, *The Fatal Lure of Politics: The Life and Thought of Vere Gordon Childe*, Monash University Publishing, Melbourne, 2020, p. 89.

8   See Ken Turner, "William John McKell" in David Clune and Ken Turner, (eds), *The Premiers of New South Wales, 1856-2005*, Vol 2, Federation Press, Sydney, 2006, pp. 256-7.

9   *The Bulletin*, 29 August 1978.

10 Figures are from David Clune, "The State Labor Party's Electoral Record in Rural New South Wales, 1904-1981", *Labour History*, No 47, November 1984, p. 92.

11 *Daily Telegraph*, 27 April 1941.

12 *Sydney Morning Herald*, 1 May 1941

13 One Country Labor candidate, George Enticknap, was elected in Murrumbidgee but soon joined the Official Party.

14 *ALP (New South Wales), Five Critical Years: The Story of the McKell Labor Government in New South Wales*, NSW Government Printer,

Sydney, 1946, pp. 5-6.

[15] NG Butlin, *Australian Domestic Product, Investment and Foreign Borrowing 1861-1938/39*, Cambridge University Press, Cambridge, 1962, p. 393.

[16] David Clune and Gareth Griffith, *Decision and Deliberation: The Parliament of New South Wales, 1856-2003*, Federation Press, Sydney, 2006, pp. 316-8.

[17] *Daily Telegraph*, 18 September 1940.

[18] Labor Policy Speech 1941 Election, 21 April 1941.

[19] *Ibid*.

[20] UAP Policy Speech 1941 Election, 22 April 1941.

[21] Don Aitkin, *The Colonel: A Political Biography of Sir Michael Bruxner*, ANU Press, Canberra, 1969, p. 243.

[22] *Daily Telegraph*, 9 May 1941.

[23] *Ibid*.

[24] Clune, "The State Labor Party's Electoral Record in Rural New South Wales, 1904-1981", pp. 92, 96.

[25] *Sydney Morning Herald*, 12 May 1941.

[26] *Daily Telegraph*, 3 June 1944.

[27] State Archives of New South Wales, Premier's Department Records, Cabinet Documents, 9/3036, 19 May 1941.

[28] Turner, "William John McKell", p. 268.

[29] David Clune, "The McKell Style of Government" in Michael Easson, (ed), *McKell: The Achievements of Sir William McKell*, Allen and Unwin, Sydney, 1988, pp. 147-8.

[30] *Ibid*.

[31] Ross Curnow, "Wurth, Wallace Charles (1896–1960)", *Australian Dictionary of Biography*, National Centre of Biography, Australian National University, https://adb.anu.edu.au/biography/wurth-wallace-charles-12080/text21673, published first in hardcopy 2002, accessed online 15 March 2021.

[32] Vince Kelly, *A Man of the People: From Boilermaker to Governor-General*, Alpha Books, Sydney, 1971, pp. 103, 158.

[33] Downing interviews.

[34] David Clune, "Reg Downing: A Safe Pair of Hands", in K Turner and M Hogan, (eds), *The Worldly Art of Politics*, Federation Press, Sydney, 2006, p. 233.

[35] Turner, "William John McKell", pp. 264-5.

[36] See Clune and Griffith, *Decision and Deliberation: The Parliament of New South Wales, 1856-2003*, pp. 361-5.

[37] *New South Wales Parliamentary Debates*, 13 April 1944, pp. 2374-5.

[38] *New South Wales Parliamentary Debates*, 19 November 1941, p. 2585.

[39] *New South Wales Parliamentary Debates*, 16 December 1943, p. 1399.

[40] *New South Wales Parliamentary Debates*, 11 November 1942, p. 872

[41] *New South Wales Parliamentary Debates*, 13 April 1944, p. 2376.

[42] Clune and Griffith, *Decision and Deliberation: The Parliament of New South Wales, 1856-2003*, p. 380. Labor achieved a majority in the Legislative Council for the first time in 1949.

[43] Clune, "Reg Downing: A Safe Pair of Hands", p. 233.

[44] Clune and Griffith, *Decision and Deliberation: The Parliament of New South Wales, 1856-2003*, pp. 375-88.

[45] Turner, "William John McKell", p. 269.

[46] Labor Policy Speech 1944 Election, 10 May 1944.

47 Ibid.

48 Ibid.

49 John McCarthy, "Bertram Sydney Barnsdale Stevens" in Clune and Turner, (eds), *The Premiers of New South Wales, 1856-2005*, p. 225.

50 Democratic Party Policy Speech 1944 Election, 12 May 1944.

51 Ibid.

52 Ibid.

53 *Daily Telegraph*, 15 January 1947.

54 Kelly, *A Man of the People: From Boilermaker to Governor-General*, p. 166.

55 Proceedings of Conference of Commonwealth and State Ministers, Canberra, 22-25 January 1946, pp. 9-11.

56 See Cunneen, *William John McKell: Boilermaker, Premier, Governor-General; and Kelly, A Man of the People: From Boilermaker to Governor-General.*

57 *Ibid.*, p. 176.

58 *Obscene and Indecent Publications (Amendment) Act 1946*, No 36.

59 John Waugh, "Appointing the Governor-General: The Case of William McKell", *Public Law Review*, Vol 17, 2006, p. 49.

60 *Sydney Morning Herald*, 15 February 1946.

61 *Ibid.*

62 14 February 1946, quoted in Paul White, "CE Martin: a political biography", unpublished MEc.thesis, University of Sydney, 1986, p. 210.

63 David Clune, "McGirr, James (Jim) (1890–1957)", *Australian*

Dictionary of Biography, National Centre of Biography, Australian National University, https://adb.anu.edu.au/biography/mcgirr-james-jim-10957/text19473, published first in hardcopy 2000, accessed online 15 March 2021.

64   A partial exception was the Cumberland town planning scheme which remained in existence while Joe Cahill was Premier (1952-59). As the minister who introduced it, Cahill retained a special regard for the scheme.

65   Philip Ayres, *Owen Dixon*, Miegunyah Press, Melbourne, 2003, p. 183.

66   See Parliament of Australia, House of Representatives Practice, 7th ed, 2018, https://www.aph.gov.au/About_Parliament/House_of_Representatives/Powers_practice_and_procedure/Practice7/HTML/Chapter13/Double_dissolutions

67   Downing interviews.

68   Cunneen, *William John McKell: Boilermaker, Premier, Governor-General*, pp. 211-12.

69   Distinguished UK constitutional lawyer, Sir Ivor Jennings, who was a member of the Commission and did most of the drafting, wrote in his diary of McKell's contribution: "He is always ready for a sensible compromise, and I was able to meet him by National Development Plans (invented by me to meet McKell's very sensible observations) and by giving some unnecessary emphasis to some of his proposals about soil conservation and so forth. The report may be thought to be to be a bit unbalanced but it does show (on McKell's insistence) that we realised the fundamental economic problems". H Kumarasingham, (ed), *Constitution-Maker: Selected Writings of Sir Ivor Jennings*, Cambridge University Press, Cambridge, 2015, p. 70.

Select Bibliography

Books and articles:

ALP (NSW), *Five Critical Years: the story of the McKell Labor Government in New South Wales*, Government Printer, Sydney, 1946.

Carr, Bob, "How moderate Labor developed its nifty style", *The Bulletin*, 29 August 1978.

Clune, David, "The NSW election of 1941", *Australian Journal of Politics and History*, Vol 30, No 3, 1984.

Clune, David, "From McKell to McGirr", *Journal of the Royal Australian Historical Society*, Vol 79, pts. 1 and 2, 1993.

Clune, David and Turner, Ken, (eds), *The Premiers of NSW, 1856-2005*, Vol 2, Federation Press, Sydney, 2006.

Cunneen, Chris, *William John McKell: Boilermaker, Premier, Governor-General*, UNSW Press, Sydney, 2000.

Easson, Michael, (ed), *McKell: The Achievements of Sir William McKell*, Allen and Unwin, Sydney, 1988.

Hogan, Michael and Clune, David, (eds), *The People's Choice: Electoral Politics in Twentieth Century NSW*, Sydney University and NSW Parliament, Vol 2, 2001.

Kelly, Vince, *A Man of the People: From Boilermaker to Governor-General*, Alpha Books, Sydney, 1971.

Nairn, Bede, "The 1916-17 Labor Party crisis in NSW and the advent of WJ McKell", *Labour History*, No 16, May 1969.

Waugh, John, "Appointing the Governor-General: the case of William McKell" *Public Law Review*, Vol 17, 2006.

Interviews:

Robert Reginald Downing: 21 November 1986, 19 December 1986; 11 September 1987, with David Clune; 10 April 1987, with David Clune and Ken Turner; 5 October 1990, with Richard Raxworthy,

William John McKell: 22 July 1977, 5 August 1977, 26 August 1977, 16 September 1977, with David Clune, Ken Turner and Heather Radi.

Election results:

The two-party preferred results for 1941 and 1944 are from Joan Rydon, "Voting in Australian Federal and State Elections 1937-61", unpublished PhD thesis, University of Melbourne, 1966. All other results are from Antony Green, "NSW Election Results 1856-2007", https://www.parliament.nsw.gov.au/electionresults18562007/

www.ingramcontent.com/pod-product-compliance
Lightning Source LLC
Chambersburg PA
CBHW060556100426
42742CB00013B/2580